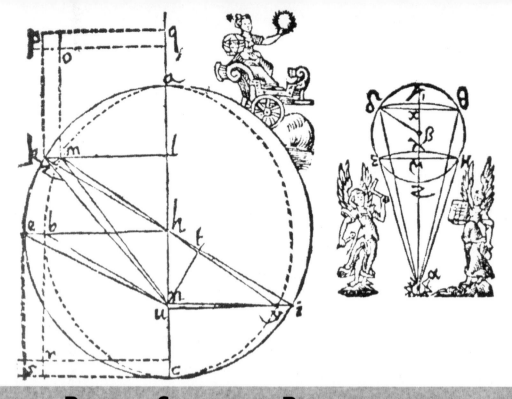

PRIMARY SOURCES OF REVOLUTIONARY
SCIENTIFIC DISCOVERIES AND THEORIES™

KEPLER AND THE LAWS OF PLANETARY MOTION

HEATHER HASAN

rosen central
Primary Source™
The Rosen Publishing Group, Inc., New York

To my sister Carrie. A more giving and self-sacrificing person you could not find.

Published in 2005 by The Rosen Publishing Group, Inc.
29 East 21st Street, New York, NY 10010

First Edition

Library of Congress Cataloging-in-Publication Data

Hasan, Heather.
Kepler and the laws of planetary motion / Heather Hasan.—1st ed.
   p. cm.—(Primary sources of revolutionary scientific discoveries and theories)
Includes bibliographical references and index.
ISBN 1-4042-0308-7 (lib. bdg.)
1. Kepler, Johannes, 1571–1630—Juvenile literature. 2. Astronomers—Germany—Biography—Juvenile literature. 3. Kepler's laws—Juvenile literature. 4. Planetary theory—Juvenile literature.
I. Title. II. Series.
QB36.K4H37 2005
520'.92—dc22

                                                                    2004007794

Printed in Hong Kong

On the front cover: Illustration of Johannes Kepler

On the back cover: Top to bottom: Nicolaus Copernicus, Charles Darwin, Edwin Hubble, Johannes Kepler, Gregor Mendel, Dmitry Mendeleyev, Isaac Newton, James Watson *(right)* and Francis Crick *(left)*

Contents

INTRODUCTION

People have been observing the movements of the planets and stars for thousands of years. For most of that time, people did not have streetlights or maps to guide their way. They only had the Moon and the bright stars that dotted the night sky with which to navigate.

THE MYSTERIOUS HEAVENS

Though we modern city dwellers may forget to look skyward and appreciate the thousands of stars that are scattered from horizon to horizon, our ancestors were fascinated by the night sky. As these ancient people observed the sky, they probably wondered about many things. How was the universe created? How old is it? How do the heavenly bodies move?

Some of the conclusions that the ancient people reached seem strange to us today. The Egyptians believed that a goddess of the heavens, Nut, had stars all over her body and stretched herself across Earth each night, forming the starry sky. She was then thought to have given birth to the Sun each morning. Until only several centuries ago, people believed that Earth was at the center of the universe. The Sun, Moon, planets, and stars were thought to have been attached to a huge sphere that rotated around Earth.

This all sounds silly to us now. We now know that the stars are large balls of hot, glowing gas that are incredibly far away. We

Johannes Kepler, shown here in this 1627 portrait, was one of the pioneers of modern astronomy. His three laws of planetary motion revolutionized the way scientists view our solar system. Kepler taught us that the planets, as well as all satellites, travel in elliptical orbits. It was previously thought that satellites travel in perfectly circular orbits. Equally important, Kepler's laws finally proved that the Sun was the center of the solar system, not Earth, as the Catholic Church had proclaimed for centuries. This new model of the known universe inspired a new way of approaching both science and religion in explaining the laws of nature.

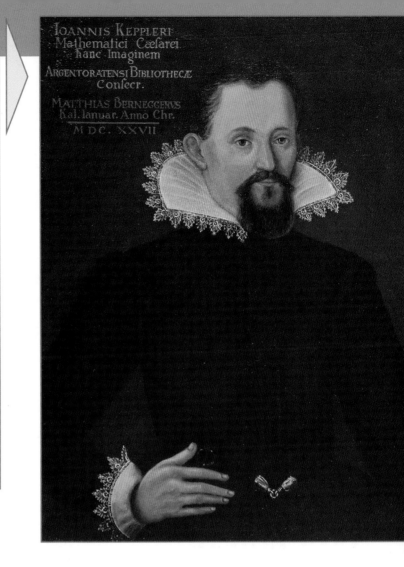

IOANNIS KEPPLERI
Mathematici Cæsarei
hanc Imaginem
ARGENTORATENSI BIBLIOTHECÆ
Confecr.
MATTHIAS BERNEGGERVS
Kal. Ianuar. Anno Chr.
MDC. XXVII

also know that the planets, including Earth, move around the Sun. Our knowledge of the laws of physics has increased so much that we are even able to send spacecraft to the farthest reaches of our solar system.

We have reached this understanding only after thousands of years of observation and the hard work and skills of past scientists who dedicated their lives to studying the planets and stars. This book tells about one such astronomer, named Johannes Kepler, and his discovery of exactly how the planets move in their orbits around the Sun.

CHAPTER 1

Johannes Kepler was born on December 27, 1571, in the small town of Weil der Stadt, in Württemburg (now part of Germany). Kepler was the first child born to Heinrich and Katherine Kepler.

Kepler had a difficult childhood. His family had once been part of the nobility. However, its property, wealth, and status had slowly dwindled away over the generations, leaving Johannes and his family poor. Heinrich Kepler deserted his family on several occasions to become a mercenary, or paid soldier, for various religious causes.

KEPLER'S LIFE

Young Johannes lived with his mother, Katherine, at his grandfather's inn. Despite his young age and poor health, he was put to work there waiting tables. He suffered from stomach problems and often got rashes and boils on his skin. Kepler was also nearsighted and had double vision. His vision problems may have been caused by a near-fatal case of smallpox from which he had suffered as a small child.

Though Kepler had a difficult childhood, he fondly recalled the dark night in 1577, when his mother woke him and brought him to a nearby hillside to introduce him to the world of astronomy. On that night, Kepler and his mother watched a comet shoot across the sky. On another night in 1580, Kepler's mother took him out on a clear night to view a lunar eclipse, the darkening of the Moon as Earth casts a shadow across it. These happy times in

Johannes Kepler was born on December 27, 1571, in the small town of Weil der Stadt, in Württemburg, which is now part of Germany. He attended college not far from there in Tübingen, Württemburg, shown here in this late nineteenth-century photograph. Kepler's road to discovery can be said to have begun here. With aspirations to become a Lutheran priest, he came to Tübingen to study theology. However, he recognized that he had other talents and pursued mathematics and astronomy instead.

an otherwise difficult childhood may have been the beginning of Kepler's life as a brilliant astronomer.

Kepler's Early Education

Despite having had a difficult youth, Kepler was obviously a gifted child. Even at an early age, his high intelligence was apparent to everyone. When Kepler's family left Weil der Stadt and moved to the nearby town of Leonberg, young Kepler was provided with greater educational opportunity. He attended the German

Schreibschule in Leonberg until his teachers realized that he was much brighter than the rest of the boys there.

He was then sent to a Latin school, designed to prepare him for the university. At the Latin school, Kepler's instructors taught him so well that for the rest of his life, he spoke and wrote clearly and beautifully in Latin. His German, however, was clumsy and confused.

Though Kepler was a brilliant student, his progress was slowed by his difficult home life. He missed a year of school when his father returned for a brief time, temporarily moving the family to a nearby village. His father then left home for the last time when Kepler was five and is said to have died somewhere in the Netherlands.

Kepler then missed another year of school when his grandfather decided that the boy had received enough education and put him to work as a dishwasher. Thankfully, Kepler's teachers recognized his intellectual potential and begged his grandfather to let him return to school.

Kepler, however, was not always well liked by his classmates. They considered him a know-it-all. He was also fiercely competitive. Nothing angered or saddened him more than the thought that one of his classmates had academically outdone him. Occasionally, his outbursts led to fistfights with the other boys.

Though Kepler often described himself in a negative way, he was a hardworking boy who had a great thirst for knowledge. He also had a deep religious faith. At the Latin school in Leonberg, Kepler prepared for a career as a clergyman in the church. Then, in 1584, when he was just thirteen, he decided to continue his clerical training by enrolling in the Adelberg convent school. He was given free room and board, which allowed him to finally escape his distracting household. Then, in 1589, he enrolled at the University of Tübingen.

Kepler's University Education

Kepler entered the University of Tübingen hoping to become a Lutheran priest. He studied philosophy and theology (the study of religion). However, Kepler excelled in mathematics, which, at that time, included astronomy.

The late sixteenth century was an exciting time to be studying astronomy, and Kepler was fortunate that one of the most respected astronomy teachers in Europe was working at the University of Tübingen. This man's name was Michael Maestlin.

Maestlin had written a textbook that was based upon the work of Claudius Ptolemy, a Greek mathematician and astronomer who lived in the second century AD in Alexandria, Egypt. Ptolemy believed that the Sun, Moon, and stars revolved around Earth, which is called the geocentric (Earth-centered) model. Part of Ptolemy's reasoning was that if Earth traveled around the Sun, everything on Earth's surface would fly off. Ptolemy had developed this theory from the teachings of the fourth-century BC Greek philosopher Aristotle. Aristotle believed that the Sun and the other known planets revolved around a stationary Earth and that Earth was made up of only four elements: earth, fire, water, and air.

Maestlin used his textbook, based on the ideas of Ptolemy to teach his students. However, outside his classroom, Maestlin privately told his students about the theory of Polish astronomer Nicolaus Copernicus (1473–1543).

The theories of Copernicus had a profound impact on Kepler's later work. Copernicus, who wrote a book titled *De Revolutionibus Orbium Coelestium* (On the Revolution of the Celestial Spheres;

MICHAEL MŒSTLINUS.
Matheseos Prof. Tubing

1543), believed that Earth and the other known planets revolved around the Sun, called the heliocentric (Sun-centered) model. He also believed that Earth made a complete spin, or rotation, on its axis once a day. Many religious men rejected Copernicus's ideas. The religious men of that time had adopted Aristotle's ideas. Anything that went against this was considered heresy since they claimed that the Catholic religion said that Earth was the center of the universe. Kepler, however, was delighted by Copernicus's ideas, and he immediately accepted them as true. Despite his interest in theology, Kepler became more and more fascinated by the idea that the planets revolved around the Sun instead of Earth.

Shown here is a diagram of the model of the universe established by Nicolaus Copernicus. This page comes from Copernicus's most important work, *De Revolutionibus Orbium Coelestium*, which was published in 1543, just before he died. The diagram shows the Sun at the center with the planets orbiting around it. The heliocentric model of the universe was revolutionary in the mid-sixteenth century. Not only did it go against the centuries-old geocentric model, it also went against the doctrine of the Catholic Church. Kepler would not only build upon Copernicus's heliocentric model, he would also prove it to be correct. (See page 54 for an excerpt.)

Teaching in Graz

As Kepler was finishing his education in Tübingen, he made an important decision that would change the direction of his life and the course of history. Kepler was selected by his teachers at the University of Tübingen to go to Graz, now part of Austria. There he would teach mathematics at a small school. Kepler had always wanted to become a priest, but upon Maestlin's urgings, he accepted the teaching position. At the age of twenty-three, Kepler abandoned his dream of becoming a priest and began a career in the study of science.

In Graz, Kepler no longer had to devote so much time to theological studies. He was free to explore all of the scientific ideas that had so excited him when he was at the University of Tübingen. He asked questions about the universe that other people took for granted. He wanted to know what the universe was made of. He also wanted to know why there were only six planets. (At the time, only Mercury, Venus, Earth, Mars, Jupiter, and Saturn were known to exist.) Further, Kepler wanted to know why the planets are situated where they are in the sky. He questioned what determines the distance between their orbits.

Kepler's questions may have seemed foolish to the scientists of his time, who were fully devoted to the theories of Aristotle. However, his questions forever changed the world of science.

CHAPTER 2

Kepler lived in a time of great religious conflict. During his lifetime, Germany and most of Europe were ruled by a Catholic emperor. People did not have religious freedom. Many times, people were required to follow the religion of their ruler. But this religious conflict in Europe began well before Kepler was born.

KEPLER AND HIS TIMES

It started in 1517, when Martin Luther (1483–1546), a German monk and teacher, posted a list of complaints against the Catholic Church on the door of a church in Wittenberg, Germany. This began what is known as the Protestant Reformation, and the reformers became known as Protestants.

The Protestants believed that the Roman Catholic Church was corrupt and needed to be changed. They were particularly displeased with the fact that priests and monks frequently sold forgiveness to the people. Luther and others like him believed that sin was forgiven through faith in God's grace alone, not by anything that people could do, such as performing good deeds or giving money.

Luther's protest spread rapidly and split Europe into two groups: Catholics and Protestants. These groups bitterly opposed each other. Years of religious violence followed. The violence

Politics, religion, and science were closely tied during Kepler's time. It can be argued that Kepler's laws of planetary motion were at risk of never being discovered as a result of the political and religious turmoil during Kepler's formative years as a scientist. Shown here is the painting *The Edict of Charles V* by the nineteenth-century artist Jan August Hendrik Leys. The painting shows Holy Roman Emperor Charles V in May 1521, outlawing Martin Luther and his followers. This edict was issued in response to Luther's refusal to stop teaching Protestantism. The later prosecution of Protestants eventually forced Kepler from his home and teaching position in Graz under the rule of Archduke Ferdinand II.

lasted until 1555, when a compromise was reached in the Peace of Augsburg settlement. With this settlement, each prince was given the right to decide what religion (Catholicism or Protestantism) would be practiced within his state. Though an uneasy peace was established, religious warfare broke out once again during Kepler's lifetime.

The early seventeenth century saw the beginning of the Thirty Years' War (1618–1648), a German civil war, which soon involved nearly all of Europe. This war resulted in the devastation of large areas of central Europe and the death of one-third of its population. This religious unrest greatly affected Kepler's life and work.

Religious Persecution

The city of Tübingen devoutly followed Luther's ideas. When Kepler moved to Graz to teach, however, he found a much more divided religious atmosphere. In Graz, Catholics and Protestants lived side by side, and this led to a lot of religious conflict.

While Kepler was living in Graz, Archduke Ferdinand II assumed rule over inner Austria, which included Graz. While Ferdinand's father had tolerated Protestants in his lands, Ferdinand II would not. Archduke Ferdinand II sought to restore Catholic domination in Europe.

Under his rule began what was called the Counter-Reformation, a movement that fought to stop the spread of Protestantism. Life was made difficult for the Protestants who were living in Graz. Eventually, the Lutheran school where Kepler taught was closed, and he and the other Protestant teachers were forced from the city on threat of death.

Though Kepler was initially allowed to return to Graz, he was later kicked out for good when he refused to convert from Protestantism to Catholicism. It was this religious persecution that brought Kepler into the company of Tycho Brahe (1546–1601), a well-known Danish astronomer of the time. Having been relieved of his teaching job in Graz, Kepler readily accepted Brahe's offer to join him in his work in Prague. The work that Kepler did with Brahe would ultimately lead to Kepler's discovery of the laws of planetary motion.

Along with Kepler's university professor Michael Maestlin, Danish astronomer Tycho Brahe was among the most influential people in the scientist's life. Brahe, shown here in this 1586 illustration, was a colorful figure to say the least. As the story goes, he once challenged a fellow student to a duel over a disagreement concerning a mathematical problem. This duel resulted in Brahe's nose being partially severed, which the illustration shows. By some accounts, Brahe wore a gold and silver replacement nose, which he would continually polish with oil. Brahe mapped the positions of the celestial bodies with the greatest precision of his time and devised a system of the universe that rejected all those that came before it.

Harmony and Witchcraft

Kepler was a very religious man. He converted to Protestantism at a very young age. Though he ultimately abandoned his dream of becoming a priest, his religious devotion greatly affected his work. He thought it was his religious duty to work toward understanding the universe that God had created. He made references to God throughout his writing. He was convinced that God had created the universe according to a mathematical plan. This belief can also be seen in the works of Plato and Pythagoras. Kepler believed that a universe that had been created by such an intelligent God would have to be one

Despite the great strides in science that were taking place during Kepler's time, superstitions that had no scientific backing continued to flourish, as shown in this fifteenth-century illustration titled "Witches Leaving for the Sabbath." The religious zeal of the time spread fear that witches did, in fact, exist. If anyone was even suspected of practicing witchcraft, he or she could be punished by execution. Kepler's own mother was even accused of the crime. As a result, Kepler had to petition the courts to free his mother of the accusation. He was eventually able to convince the courts to drop the charges. It is ironic that one of history's greatest scientific minds had to clear his own mother of this untested superstition.

of perfect mathematical order. He felt that the mind of God was mathematical and that the more we thought in numbers, the clearer our thinking would be.

Kepler became obsessed with finding God's harmony in nature. Perhaps it was the religious conflict of the time that led him to search the heavens for celestial harmony. Kepler believed that the heavenly bodies moved together in an orderly fashion. He even thought that the planets made sounds as they moved, the way that the strings of a lyre do as they are played. Kepler's book, *Harmonice Mundi* (Harmony of the World; 1619), demonstrates these theories. It also contains the third of his three laws of planetary motion.

While Kepler searched for harmony, however, his life was anything but harmonious. The religious zeal of the sixteenth and seventeenth centuries led to witch-hunting hysteria. People were obsessed with identifying and executing the people they suspected of being witches.

Kepler's mother, Katherine, was one of the many people charged with practicing witchcraft. Kepler came to his mother's defense, writing letters and petitioning the court to drop the charges. The trial went on for years before Katherine Kepler was finally released.

Astronomy and Astrology

Despite all of this trouble and the start of the Thirty Years' War, Kepler continued to work. While he was teaching, Kepler was also district mathematician. In this position, he surveyed the land, settled disputes over the accuracy of weights and measures used in business, and made calendars.

In addition to listing dates on his calendars, Kepler was expected to list information that was important to the people of his time. Today's calendars include some additional information, such as holidays and phases of the Moon (full, new, etc.). During Kepler's time, however, the people expected that the calendar would make predictions for their everyday lives that were based on the positions of the heavenly bodies. The study of the supposed influence of the heavenly bodies on people's lives is called astrology.

On his calendars, Kepler gave advice to farmers about when they should plant and harvest their crops. He also gave advice to military and political leaders. He even offered advice on matters of romance.

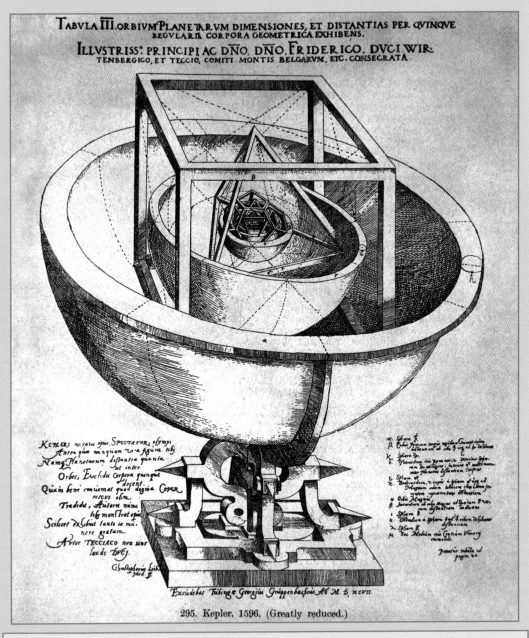

295. Kepler. 1596. (Greatly reduced.)

Using the theories of the ancient Greek scientists, Kepler fashioned an early model of how he believed the universe is constructed. He began with the theory of five Platonic solids, which are the only shapes that could fit in a sphere with each of the points of the shape touching the sphere. Kepler believed these shapes would determine the distances between each of the six known planets. Shown here is Kepler's drawing of a model of the Platonic solids he planned to build, as published in *Mysterium Cosmographicum* (Mystery of the Cosmos) in 1597.

Today we know that the positions of the Sun, Moon, and planets, along with the tilt of Earth on its axis, determine things such as the tides, the seasons of the year, the phases of the Moon, and eclipses of the Sun and Moon. These occurrences can be important to the plans of farmers and military leaders. A farmer knows that there are certain times when it is better for him to plant and harvest his crops. And a military leader may wish to plan an attack to fit in with the seasons or when there will be a certain amount of moonlight.

In the seventeenth century, there was little difference between astronomy and astrology. People had only a limited understanding of the movements of the heavenly bodies and were unsure about which events in their lives were affected by them. We are now able to understand the difference between the legitimate scientific conclusions that astronomy offers as opposed to the unfounded claims of astrology.

Kepler believed that by seeing which of his predictions were correct, he could sort out which kinds of predictions were legitimate and which ones were not. In 1602, Kepler wrote a book titled, *De Fundamentis Astrologiae Certioribus* (Concerning the More Certain Fundamentals of Astrology). In this book, he stated that he did not agree with the superstition that the stars determine what happens in people's lives. Kepler was the first person to investigate the accuracy of astrology in this way. He showed that trusting astrological predictions could be a risky thing to do!

Astronomy in the Seventeenth Century

For centuries, people believed only in Aristotle's idea that Earth sat still while the planets, the Sun, and the Moon traveled around it in circular orbits. They tried to fit their observations into his model of the universe. The people of the time believed things to be true simply because Aristotle said they were true. However, during the sixteenth century, people began to think more for themselves. They began to believe that things were true based upon their own experiences, through observation and experimentation.

It was not until the seventeenth century that science finally broke free from tradition. Kepler bravely based his explanations on what he observed. Nicolaus Copernicus, who had so greatly influenced Kepler, was one of the most revolutionary scientists in the sixteenth century. Though Copernicus believed the planets revolved around the Sun, he falsely believed they revolved in circles. Kepler respected Copernicus's ideas, but he did not try to make his observations fit into Copernicus's model of the universe.

The fact that Kepler asked questions was unique for his time. It is expected for scientists today to ask why things are the way they are instead of simply describing how they are. However, this was not the case for scientists prior to the late sixteenth century. Part of what made Kepler a genius is that he was not afraid to ask why. Kepler's radical way of thinking marked the beginning of modern scientific astronomy.

CHAPTER 3

Copernicus had been dead for fifty years when Kepler was introduced to his ideas at the University of Tübingen. Kepler read Copernicus's theories in *De Revolutionibus Orbium Coelestium*, and he was immediately drawn to the book's difficult mathematical text.

Copernicus was not the first person to suggest the heliocentric model, though. The Greek writer Aristarchus proposed these ideas in the third century BC. However, they were rejected by the followers of Aristotle. It is easy to see why they were rejected. The ideas seem to go against common sense. How can Earth orbit the Sun while at the same time spin at such a dizzying speed? What keeps the things that are on Earth's surface from flying off as Earth spins? If Earth rotates on its axis, why do objects fall straight down when dropped?

STUDYING THE STARS

The religious men of the time, especially the Protestants, rejected Copernicus's ideas. The Copernican model greatly appealed to Kepler, however. Kepler believed that the Sun was God's most brilliant heavenly creation. In fact, he believed that the Sun represented God. He felt that it was only fitting, therefore, that it should be at the center of the universe, with Earth and the other planets revolving around it. He also believed that the force that drove the planets to revolve around the Sun came from the Sun itself. This faith that Kepler had in the Sun would play a big part in his later discoveries.

Kepler's First Model of the Heavens

While teaching a geometry class in Graz, Kepler had a revelation that he felt was the secret to understanding the universe. On the blackboard, Kepler drew a triangle within a circle. He then drew another circle within the triangle. It suddenly occurred to him that the ratio of the larger circle to the smaller circle was the same as the ratio of the orbits of Saturn and Jupiter. Kepler was very excited by his finding. He assumed that geometric figures would fit into the spaces between the orbits of all of the planets. He began to look for orbital patterns of the planets using other shapes.

Eventually, Kepler looked toward the Pythagorean and Platonic shapes, or "solids," that had been used by the ancient Greeks. There were only five so-called perfect solids: the tetrahedron, hexahedron, octahedron, dodecahedron, and icosahedron. These three-dimensional shapes were considered perfect because they are able to fit exactly into a sphere with all of their points touching the sphere.

Because of their "perfection," followers of the ancient Greek mathematician Pythagoras thought that these shapes actually had magical powers. To Kepler, the Platonic solids explained why there could only be six planets, the number of planets believed to exist at the time. With six planets, there would be a total of five spaces between them, one space for each Platonic solid. He felt that the distances between the Platonic solids, when fitted within one another, determined the distances between the orbits of planets. Kepler planned to build a copper model of his geometrical design, but he only succeeded in building a paper one.

Shown here is a sculpture of the sixth-century BC Greek philosopher and mathematician Pythagoras. This sculpture is a Roman copy of a Greek original. Pythagoras had great influence on Kepler's scientific development. Following the theory of the Platonic solids, which many of Pythagoras's followers believed had magical powers, Kepler built the foundation for his laws of planetary motion. These shapes were also called perfect solids. They were given this name because each shape could fit perfectly within a sphere with all of the points touching the sphere. Because these five shapes had this characteristic, it was assumed that they were unique in the universe.

Kepler was excited by his geometric theory, and he immediately began working on a book to explain his ideas. It took him a year to write the book, which he titled *Mysterium Cosmographicum* (Mystery of the Cosmos).

When the book was published in 1597, Kepler sent copies of it to Italian astronomer and mathematician Galileo Galilei (1564–1642) and Brahe, urging them to believe in his theory. Galileo rejected the theory, but Brahe was immediately intrigued by it. Brahe saw Kepler's work as exciting, and he wrote a glowing letter to Kepler in support of it. Today, Kepler's geometric theory appears bizarre. However, though Kepler's conclusions

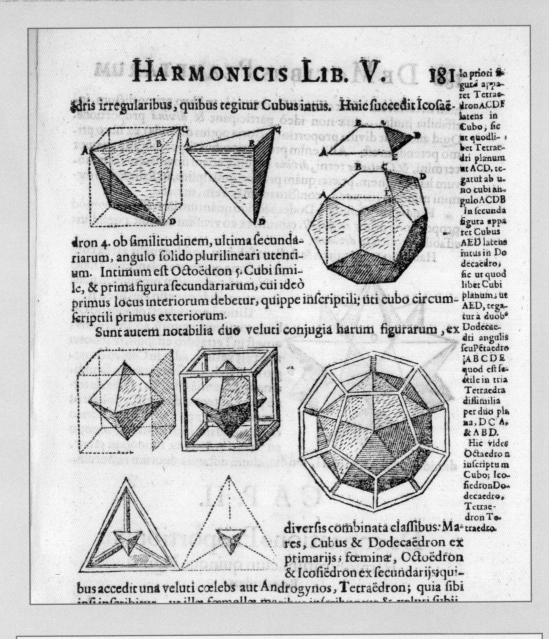

Kepler became obsessed with finding harmony in the universe. Shown here is page 181 from his book *Harmonice Mundi* (Harmony of the World), published in 1619. The illustration is an example of Kepler's quest to discover numerous sets of polyhedra (shapes with multiple sides). Kepler believed that many of nature's mysteries could be found in the mathematics of polyhedra. He used these shapes, for example, in the form of Platonic solids. Using the Platonic solids, he developed his theory, which was later proved wrong, that the measurements of the solids could be used to calculate the distances between the planets. (See page 54 for an excerpt.)

were later proved to be incorrect, the reaction he received from Brahe changed the direction of his life.

An Invitation That Changed History

Brahe was one of the best astronomers of the time. He was well known for the accuracy with which he calculated the changing positions of the Moon, Mars, and other planets. However, Kepler did not agree with Brahe's model of the universe. Brahe rejected both Ptolemy's and Copernicus's views of the universe and had produced his own system, which he called the Tychonic system.

Brahe correctly believed that the other planets orbited the Sun and that the Moon orbited Earth. However, like Ptolemy, Brahe thought that the Sun and the stars revolved around Earth. Though Kepler did not have a lot of respect for Brahe's conclusions, he longed to get his hands on the detailed data that Brahe had carefully gathered over the previous twenty years of the changing positions of the Moon, Mars, and other planets. With it, Kepler hoped to create a new model of the solar system.

Brahe had become interested in Kepler when he read *Mysterium Cosmographicum*. He called Kepler's work brilliant and felt that Kepler would be very useful in interpreting some of the data he had collected. Brahe, though a skillful observer, did not quite know what to do with his observations. Kepler was thrilled when he received Brahe's letter praising his work. He was also in need of employment since his school in Graz had closed. In 1600, Brahe invited Kepler to come to Prague, a town not far from Graz, to work with him. This invitation would change history.

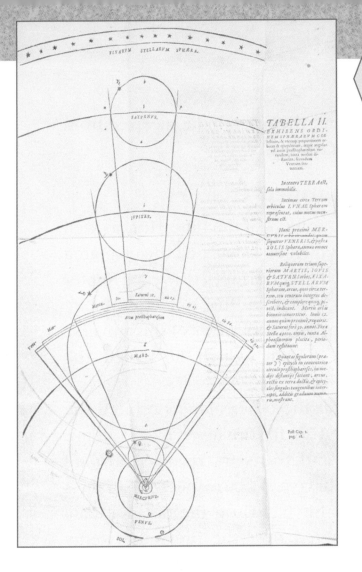

Working with Brahe

Brahe's observatory was in the Castle of Benatek, near Prague. In the observatory, he had many instruments with which to observe the sky. His instruments differed from those that are used by today's astronomers, but they were the finest of the time. Since telescopes had not yet been invented, scientists had to rely on quadrants, large instruments used for determining the heights of stars and planets. In his observatory, Brahe also had giant wood and metal sextants. These devices were used to measure the angle between two objects, such as planets or stars. Brahe also had a great armillary sphere, which he used to obtain

Shown here is the terrace of Belvedere Castle in Prague, Czech Republic. The castle was used, in addition to the Castle of Benatek, by Johannes Kepler and Tycho Brahe when they worked together. The instruments shown are two quadrants and a globe sitting on the ledge. The quadrants were used to measure altitudes. From the information the scientists gathered from the quadrants, they were able to chart the positions of the planets and the stars. The result of their calculations was the most complete star map of the day: the Rudolphine tables.

the positions of stars. Also in the observatory was a magnificent brass globe on which Brahe had engraved the results of his careful observations, the positions of a thousand stars.

Kepler and Brahe had a rocky relationship. When Kepler agreed to go to Prague, he thought he would be treated as an equal to Brahe. However, Kepler was instead treated as a servant. Before coming to Prague, Kepler had dreamt of having access to Brahe's data. However, Brahe was mistrustful of Kepler, and he refused to share any of his data with him.

Finally, however, Brahe decided to give Kepler an assignment. Brahe's life dream was to be known for generations to come as the man who had set the course for future astronomy. As he grew older, he saw that dream slipping away, and he felt that he was approaching death. He did not want his data to go to waste, so he decided to take a chance with Kepler. Brahe recognized Kepler's gift for mathematics and his ability to apply mathematics to astronomy. He thought that Kepler would perhaps be able to make sense of his observations of Mars, the orbit of which he had difficulty fitting into his calculations. He also thought that Kepler would be able to prove that his Tychonic system was correct. This was the beginning of Kepler's road to discovering the laws of planetary motion.

CHAPTER 4

Kepler struggled with the data for Mars. He had been given the task of figuring out what path, or orbit, Mars took as it revolved around the Sun. This process would prove to be quite difficult. An example of Kepler's exhaustive work is the nearly 1,000 folio sheets of his data that survive today.

THE SERVANT BECOMES THE MASTER

Some scientists believe that part of the reason that Brahe gave the Mars problem to Kepler was that he was hoping its difficulty would keep Kepler occupied while he worked on his own theory of the solar system. If this is true, it is quite funny that it was precisely the data for Mars that allowed Kepler to develop his laws of planetary motion. Kepler's discovery would also disprove Brahe's system and give Kepler the place in astronomy's history that Brahe had wanted for himself.

Though Brahe had allowed Kepler to see the data for Mars, his distrust of Kepler kept him from sharing his observations of the Moon and other planets with Kepler. This frustrated Kepler, who felt he needed all of Brahe's data in order to reach a conclusion. However, he was able to make some progress with the little data he had.

Named after Roman emperor Rudolph II, Johannes Kepler's *Rudolphine Tables* (1627) was the most reliable book by which the positions of the planets and the stars could be studied. Shown here is the frontispiece illustration of *Rudolphine Tables*, which depicts a temple built on the foundations of the works of great astronomers of history until Kepler's time. Kepler himself is pictured in the panel at the bottom left. Kepler's tables were about thirty times more complete than any previous ones. *Rudolphine Tables* was also the first book to require the use of logarithms, which had recently been invented by John Napier. Kepler used the tables to predict the passing of the planet Mercury between Earth and the Sun, which was observed by Pierre Gassendi in 1631. This prediction further proved that Sun is the center of the solar system.

Kepler focused on his theory that a force from the Sun moves the planets—what we now know is gravity. First, he concluded that Mars's orbit only made sense if the Sun was the source of its motion. Next, Kepler creatively used the observations of Mars to study Earth's orbit. He found that Earth, like the other planets, sped up as it neared the Sun and slowed down as it got farther away. In a time when many people wanted to believe that Earth, in all its importance, was the center of the universe, Kepler had discovered that Earth moved just like the other planets. This was a significant breakthrough, though it would be years before Kepler would finish his battle with Mars.

Obtaining Brahe's Data

One of Brahe's greatest fears was that his life would be meaningless. Fearing that he did not have much longer to live and wanting to prove his Tychonic system, he finally made a monumental decision. He decided to give Kepler the task of putting together new tables of astronomical data that would be based on his superb observations and would be published as *Rudolphine Tables*.

Other astronomical tables had been written in the past, but the Rudolphine tables, named after the Roman emperor Rudolph II, would be the most accurate ones the world had ever known. When finished, the Rudolphine tables would be useful for figuring out the positions of the planets 1,000 years into the past and 1,000 years into the future. Brahe's decision to have Kepler work on the Rudolphine tables was an important decision in the history of science. It gave Kepler access to all of Brahe's data, which he desperately needed to come up with the laws of planetary motion.

Only a few weeks after Kepler began his work on the Rudolphine tables, Brahe died in 1601. Soon after Brahe's death,

Emperor Rudolph II named Kepler the new imperial mathematician (a position that Brahe had previously held). As the imperial mathematician, Kepler was put in charge of Brahe's instruments, his writings, and the Rudolphine tables. Brahe's full set of observations had finally fallen into Kepler's hands. Kepler used the data to finish and publish *Rudolphine Tables* in 1627, but not before he completed his work with Mars.

Kepler's Elliptical Orbits

By 1604, Kepler was still trying to solve the riddle of Mars's orbit. Kepler had examined Brahe's data for years. He knew that Brahe's measurements were accurate because he had watched him and his assistants at the Prague observatory making and double-checking their observations. However, when Kepler plotted out all of the locations at which Brahe had observed Mars over the years, he noticed that the data did not fit its orbit into a circular path. The idea that the planets traveled in circular paths was universally accepted in Kepler's time. When he began the project, Kepler himself had been convinced that Mars's orbit was circular. However, no amount of adjusting made his figures work for a circular orbit.

It was at that point that Kepler used an insight and an imagination that had rarely been matched in the history of science. He finally began to question circular orbits. Turning away from popular thinking, Kepler tried different orbital paths to see which shape would work. When he tried an oval, or ellipse, he felt as though he had been awakened from a deep sleep. It worked!

Kepler put the conclusions he had reached while working with Mars into a book called *Astronomia Nova* (New Astronomy).

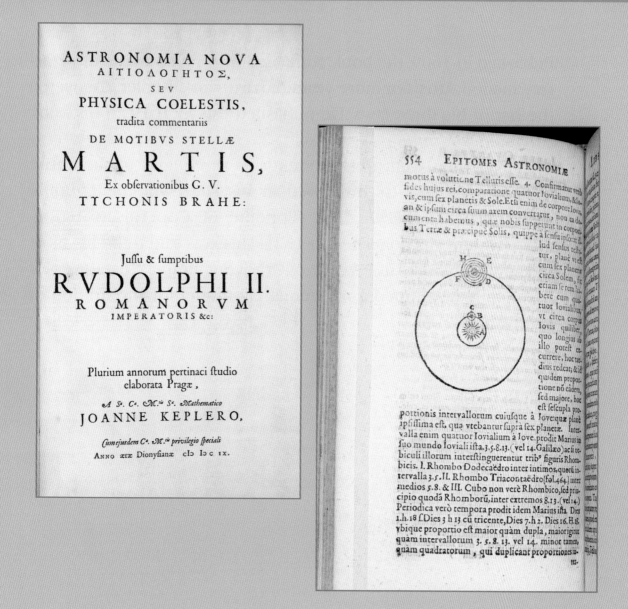

The first account of the planets having elliptical rather than circular orbits was published in 1609 in Kepler's *Astronomia Nova* (New Astronomy), the title page of which is shown here *(left)*. Not only is the book a testament to Kepler's mathematical genius, it is also an example of his powers of imagination. Unable to calculate the circular orbit of Mars, he experimented with other orbital shapes. One of these shapes, of course, was the ellipse, which fit into his calculations. Shown at right is a page from book four of Kepler's seven-volume *Epitome Astronomiae Copernicanae* (Epitome of Copernican Astronomy), published in 1621. Here, Kepler applies his third law of planetary motion to infer the dimensions of the orbits of the Galilean moons of Jupiter. (See page 55 for an excerpt.)

Published in 1609, the book contained his first two laws of planetary motion. After ten more years of hard work, Kepler discovered the last of his three laws. He published this in 1619, in his book *Harmonice Mundi*.

Kepler then went on to extend his three laws to the entire solar system. This he described in his seven-volume *Epitome Astronomiae Copernicanae* (Epitome of Copernican Astronomy), which was published in 1621. This was said to be his most influential work. After years of studying Brahe's data, Kepler had finally developed a mathematical model for the motion of the planets.

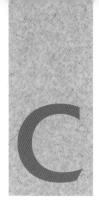

CHAPTER 5

Kepler's key discoveries are known today as Kepler's laws of planetary motion. Kepler's first law is known as the law of ellipses. This law describes the shape of the path that the planets take as they travel around the Sun. It states that each planet moves around the Sun in an elliptical orbit, with the Sun standing at one focus of the ellipse.

Kepler's second law is referred to as the law of equal areas. This law describes how fast a planet moves along its orbit. It states that the imaginary line joining each planet to the Sun (called the radius vector) sweeps through equal areas of space in equal amounts of time as the planet moves along its orbital path.

UNDERSTANDING KEPLER'S LAWS

Finally, Kepler's third law, the one that was described in his book *Harmonice Mundi*, is known as the harmonic law. This law describes the relationship between the orbital period of a planet and its distance from the Sun. It states that the square of a planet's orbital period around the Sun is directly proportional to the cube of the planet's mean, or average, distance from the Sun.

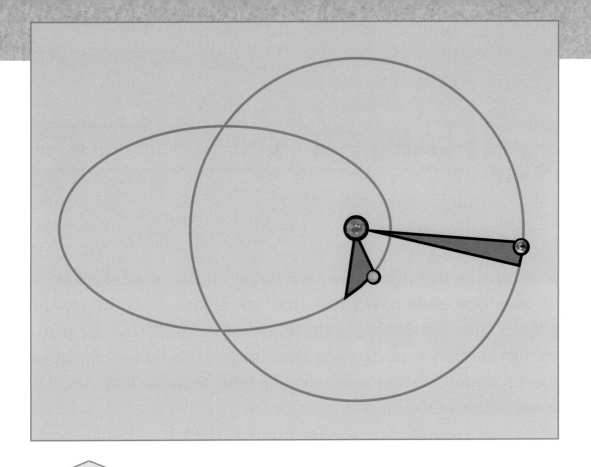

Kepler's first law of planetary motion, the law of ellipses, simply states that the paths of the orbits of the planets are ellipses with the Sun at one focus. This illustration shows both an elliptical orbit and a circular one. Unlike the circular orbit with the focus at the center, the ellipse has its focus located at the far right. This means that the distances between the planets and the Sun change as the planets travel around their orbits.

Kepler's First Law: The Law of Ellipses

What is an ellipse? An ellipse is a special type of oval. You can draw your own ellipse by using two thumbtacks, a pencil, and a piece of string with its ends tied together. If the string is looped around the two thumbtacks and the pencil, and it is pulled tight, the pencil will trace out an ellipse. The planet with the least elliptical orbit is Venus, followed by Neptune and Earth. The most elliptical orbit belongs to Pluto, followed by Mercury and Mars.

Though the orbits of the planets that were known of in Kepler's time are ellipses, they are very nearly circles. Of the planets that were known, Mars had one of the most elliptical orbits. The orbits of most of the other planets seemed to conform to a circular path, but Mars, being more elliptical, did not. That is why it was so difficult for Kepler to solve the shape of Mars's orbital path. He had to give up the idea that planets traveled in circular paths.

The shortest diameter, or distance from opposite sides through a focus across an ellipse, is called the minor axis. The longest diameter across an ellipse is called the major axis. An ellipse has two foci. This means that it has two centers, unlike a circle, which has just one. These are represented by the two thumbtacks. The foci are located along the major axis. The sum of the distances from from one focus to any point on the ellipse and to the other focus is constant. This means that it is always the same. The greater the distance between the two foci, the more elongated the ellipse. If the two foci are brought together until they join, the ellipse becomes a circle.

The Sun is located at one of the foci, or one focus, of the ellipse, not in the center. Each planet follows the ellipse in its orbit. Therefore, the distance between the planet and the Sun changes as the planet moves along its elliptical orbit.

The point at which a planet is nearest to the Sun is called the perihelion, and the point at which a planet is farthest from the Sun is called the aphelion. Earth is at its closest to the Sun in January, and it is the farthest away in July.

Kepler's Second Law: The Law of Equal Areas

The second law of planetary motion states that planets do not move at a uniform, or constant, speed. The speed of each planet

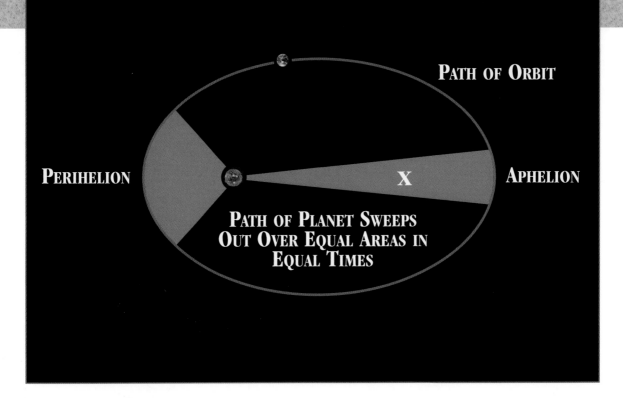

PATH OF ORBIT

PERIHELION

X

APHELION

PATH OF PLANET SWEEPS
OUT OVER EQUAL AREAS IN
EQUAL TIMES

Kepler's second law, known as the law of equal areas, is illustrated here. Just as the distances between the planets and the Sun change as the planets travel around their orbits, so do their speeds. As the planets move farther away from the Sun, they slow down. As they move closer to the Sun, they speed up. What does remain constant, however, is the area in the triangles highlighted in the illustration. The width of each triangle is the distance the planet travels around its orbit over a period of time. Where the planet is closer to the Sun, it travels over a farther distance during the period of time. Where the planet is farther away, it travels over a shorter distance during the same period of time. This means that the closer the planet is to the Sun, the faster it travels. The farther it is, the slower it travels.

changes as it orbits the Sun, going faster when it is closer to the Sun and slower when farther away.

Imagine a planet traveling around the Sun in an elliptical orbit. Draw a straight line from the Sun to the planet. Wait a minute as the planet continues to move, and then draw another line from the Sun to the planet. You would have drawn what looks like a pie wedge. Kepler showed that pie wedges created at one-minute intervals will all have the same area. Area can be measured in different units, such as square feet, square inches, or square meters.

Though the wedges created during the one-minute intervals as a planet travels around the Sun would have the same area, they would not be the same shape. Because the planets move faster when they are closer to the Sun, they are able to travel farther along the elliptical path during a one-minute interval than they can when they are farther away from the Sun. Therefore, when a planet is nearer to the Sun, the wedges created during the one-minute interval would be wider and shorter than those created when the planet is farther away. When the planet is farther away, the wedge created during a one-minute interval would be thinner and longer, and the planet would only cover a small part of the orbital path.

Though the pie wedges are different shapes, they take up the same amount of space because one is short and wide and the other is long and thin. Though the speed of a planet changes as it orbits the Sun, this speed varies at predictable rates. This is described by the third law of planetary motion.

Kepler's Third Law: The Harmonic Law

The orbital period is the time it takes for a planet to make one full orbit around the Sun. Kepler's third law shows that orbital period (time) and distance are related to each other mathematically. Kepler discovered that the square of a planet's orbital period around the Sun is directly proportional to the cube of the planet's mean distance from the Sun.

Many times, scientists describe a planet's mean distance from the Sun in astronomical units (AU). One AU is equal to 92,961,440

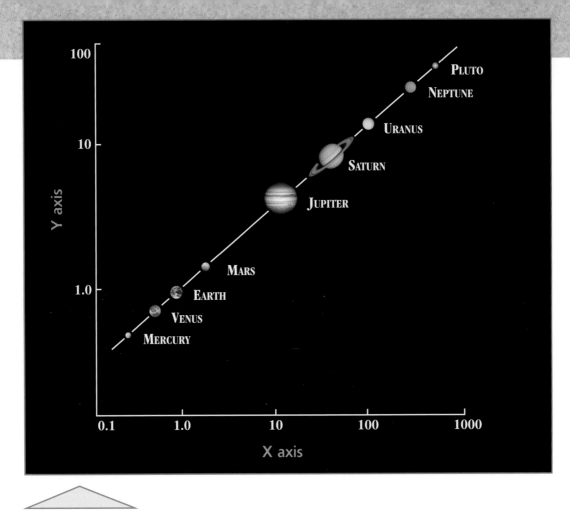

Kepler's third law of planetary motion, the harmonic law, states that the time period and distance of a planet's orbit are proportional to one another. Specifically, the square of a planet's orbital period is directly proportional to the cube of its mean distance from the Sun. As this graph shows, each of the nine planets' distance from the Sun, the "semi-major axis" and orbital period, the "sidereal period," are equal. This is why all the planets fall along the same line in the graph.

miles (149,606,936 km), which is Earth's mean distance from the Sun. Astronomical units make scientists' lives easier, because, when scientists use them, they don't have to work with such big numbers. Instead of saying that Earth is 92,961,440 miles (149,606,936 km) from the Sun, they can just say it is one AU from the Sun. In the same way, instead of saying that Jupiter is 483,399,488 miles (777,956,650 km) from the Sun, they can say it is 5.2 AU from the Sun.

Kepler's third law can be written out in a mathematical equation:

$$P^2 = d^3$$

Here, P represents a planet's orbital period, the time in years that it takes for the planet to orbit. The d represents the planet's average distance (in astronomical units) from the Sun.

In this equation, the orbital period (P) is squared. The square of a number is that number multiplied by itself. In other words: P times P. In the equation, the distance (d) is cubed. This means d times d times d.

This equation tells us that the length of a planet's year depends on its mean distance from the Sun. A planet that is closer to the Sun moves faster than one that is farther from the Sun. Therefore, it takes less time for a planet that is closer to the Sun to get around it once than it does for a planet that is farther away.

Mercury, which is only 0.39 AU from the Sun, speeds around it in only eighty-eight days. Earth takes one year, but Mars, which is at a distance of 1.52 AU, takes almost two years. Pluto, the farthest planet from the Sun, takes almost 250 years to travel around the Sun just one time!

CHAPTER 6

Kepler was not only the first person to correctly explain planetary motion, but he is also credited with a lot of "firsts" in the field of optics. Optics is the science of light. In 1604, Kepler published a book entitled *Astronomiae Pars Optica* (The Optical Part of Astronomy). In it, he described many of his discoveries in optics.

THE WORLD SINCE KEPLER

Kepler was the first person to investigate the formation of pictures with a device called a pinhole camera. Kepler was also the first person to correctly explain how an image is formed in the human eye. He discovered that the objects we see are projected upside down and backward on the retina, the back part of the eye.

He also was the first to figure out how to use differently shaped eyeglasses to correct nearsightedness (difficulty seeing objects that are far away) and farsightedness (difficulty seeing objects that are close up). This topic was an especially personal one for Kepler, who wore spectacles himself.

Kepler was the first person to explain that an image in the human eye is projected upside down on the back of the retina, the same way it is projected in a pinhole camera. Shown here are Kepler's illustrations of the human eyeball, as published in his *Astronomiae Pars Optica* (The Optical Part of Astronomy) in 1604.

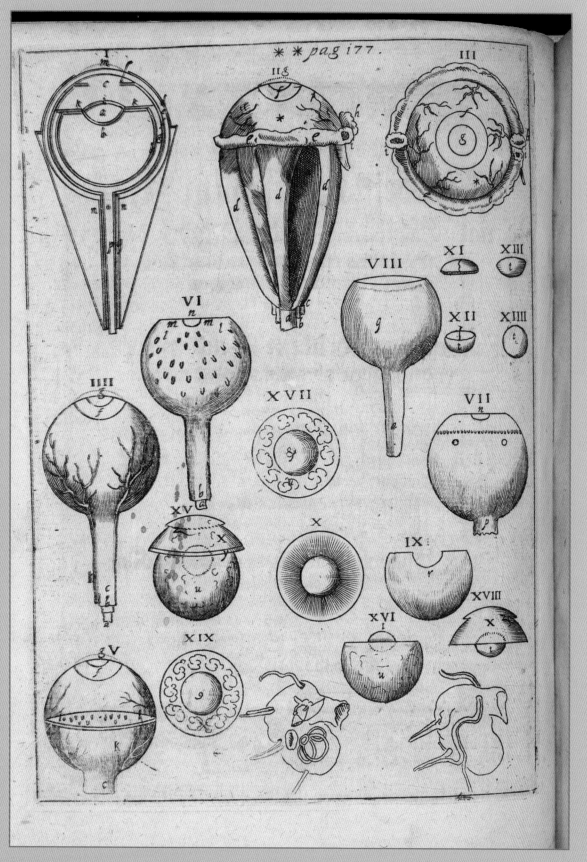

Kepler's genius reached far beyond astronomy. He was also an expert in optics, the science of light. Kepler was one of the pioneers of photography. Though he didn't invent the pinhole camera, shown here in this illustration by the sixteenth-century natural philosopher Giambattista della Porta, he was one of the first to explain how it worked. What he found was that the camera projects images upside down and backward when light passes through its lens in the same way that images are projected upside down and backward on the retina of the eye.

Kepler later applied the ideas from *Astronomiae Pars Optica* to the telescope. He described this work in his book *Dioptrice* (Dioptrics; 1611). Though Kepler did not invent the telescope, he was the first to explain the principles of how the telescope works. Inside a telescope are many lenses and mirrors that gather light and allow people to observe objects that are very far away. Kepler's work began the new field of science called dioptrics, the science of refraction by lenses. (Refraction is the turning or bending of light.) The idea of dioptrics was later used by other scientists to better understand the function of the eye and to make improvements on the telescope.

Kepler's Influence on Newton

In pondering why the planets changed speed as they revolved around the Sun, Kepler decided that the Sun exerts some kind of force on the planets that diminishes as the planets get farther away from the Sun. This laid the foundation for the discovery of the principles of gravity.

Although Kepler explained how the planets move around the Sun, he did not completely understand the force that makes them move. The principles of gravity were later explained by the English scientist Isaac Newton (1642–1727) in the 1600s. Newton discovered that objects attract each other by gravitation. He showed that the more massive an object is, the harder it pulls on another object. He also realized that the farther away an object is, the less it feels the pull of the other object.

Kepler's findings were revolutionary, and they led directly to Newton's law of universal gravitation. With the laws of gravitation came understanding of why orbits are elliptical, why planets move with changing speeds, and why the outer planets move more slowly than the inner planets. Together, these two brilliant scientists gave us a better understanding of our universe.

Kepler and Math

Kepler also made many important discoveries in the field of mathematics. One of these was a method for finding the volumes of solids. Volume is the amount of space that something takes up. Kepler's inspiration to study this subject came from an odd source.

At his wedding, Kepler noticed many differently shaped wine barrels. He learned that the volumes of the barrels were estimated by measuring only their diagonal lengths. The shapes of the barrels were disregarded. Kepler wondered how that could work. His pondering led him to write *Nova Stereometria Doliorum Vinariorum* (New Solid Geometry of Wine Barrels). Though this book was not hugely popular at the time, it became a very important step in the development of integral calculus, a type of math that is used for figuring out things such as volume and area.

Kepler was a brilliant mathematician. Brahe recognized this, and that is why he chose to put Kepler in charge of his valuable observations. Using his mathematical talents, Kepler was able to unlock the secrets that were hidden in Brahe's data and produce his world-changing laws of planetary motion, as well as many other mathematical laws.

Kepler's Effect on Our Daily Lives

Though Kepler contributed to science in many ways, he is best known for his laws of planetary motion and the way in which he discovered them. Kepler's laws have a wide range of applications. In addition to the planets revolving around the Sun, Kepler's laws are obeyed by stars revolving around each other, stars orbiting within galaxies, and even galaxies revolving around other galaxies.

Kepler's laws also explain the motion of satellites. Satellites are objects, such as the Moon, that orbit Earth and other planets. When objects are sent into orbit by people, they are called artificial satellites. Artificial satellites are important for things such as weather forecasting, scientific research, and communication.

Artificial satellites follow the same laws of planetary motion as do the nine planets. With Kepler's equations, scientists are able to launch and control satellites such as this into space. Without the laws that Kepler devised, we wouldn't have such technology as satellite television or satellite radio. Neither would we have the Hubble Space Telescope, shown here, to help us view the farthest reaches of the universe.

Some artificial satellites carry instruments that gather information about Earth and its surroundings and then send it back to Earth. This information is important to scientists, military personnel, farmers, and weather forecasters, just to name a few.

The satellites called communications satellites are used to relay radio, telephone, and television signals. It is these satellites that make it possible for you to watch your favorite television shows or sporting events live. Without Kepler, none of this would be possible.

The Beginning of Modern Astronomy

Kepler's laws of planetary motion are very useful, but the way in which he discovered them is also important. Kepler used the precise data that Brahe had collected to formulate his laws of planetary motion. His discovery of these laws marked the beginning of modern astronomy.

Unlike many of the astronomers who came before him, Kepler was true to his data. When he began his work, Kepler believed that the orbits of the planets were circular. The observations that Brahe had given him, however, did not correlate with that idea. Instead of changing the data to fit his beliefs, as those who came before him often had, Kepler sought to develop explanations that would fit with the data. This was a revolutionary way of approaching scientific research, and it changed the way scientists work.

Science requires both experimentation and creativity. Johannes Kepler was skillful in both areas. He also used these skills as he tried to understand how the universe works. It is

Kepler, shown in this portrait, is considered one of the great figures in the history of science. He discovered a system by which the universe operates, just as other great scientific figures such as Nicolaus Copernicus, Isaac Newton, and Albert Einstein had. As proof of his greatness, Kepler's laws of planetary motion are still used in their original form by scientists today, nearly 400 years after his death. Without Kepler's laws of planetary motion, the world would be a very different place. Scientists wouldn't be able to launch spacecraft or communications satellites. These and other technologies will continue to be influenced by Kepler's laws of planetary motion well into the future.

for this reason that he has been referred to as the father of modern astronomy.

Johannes Kepler died in 1630. Though his grave was destroyed during the Thirty Years' War, his world-changing discoveries live on.

TIMELINE

1517	— Martin Luther begins the Protestant Reformation by posting a list of complaints against the Catholic Church.
1571	— Johannes Kepler is born on December 27.
1577	— Kepler sees his first comet.
1589	— Kepler attends the University of Tübingen.
1594	— Kepler goes to Graz to teach mathematics.
1597	— Kepler publishes *Mysterium Cosmographicum* (Mystery of the Cosmos).
1600	— Kepler goes to Prague to work with Tycho Brahe.
1601	— Brahe dies.
1602	— Kepler writes *De Fundamentis Astrologiae Certioribus* (Concerning the More Certain Fundamentals of Astrology).
1604	— Kepler publishes *Astronomiae Pars Optica* (The Optical Part of Astronomy).
1609	— Kepler publishes *Astronomia Nova* (New Astronomy).
1611	— Kepler publishes *Dioptrice* (Dioptrics).

1615	—	Kepler publishes *Nova Stereometria Doliorum Vinariorum* (New Solid Geometry of Wine Barrels).
1618	—	The Thirty Years' War begins.
1619	—	Kepler publishes *Harmonice Mundi* (Harmony of the World).
1621	—	Kepler publishes *Epitome Astronomiae Copernicanae* (Epitome of Copernican Astronomy).
1627	—	Kepler publishes *Rudolphine Tables*.
1630	—	Kepler dies on November 15.

PRIMARY SOURCE TRANSCRIPTIONS

Page 11: From *De Revolutionibus Orbium Coelestium* (On the Revolution of the Celestial Spheres)

Among the many and varied literary and artistic studies upon which the natural talents of man are nourished, I think that those above all should be embraced and pursued with the most loving care which have to do with things that are very beautiful and very worthy of knowledge. Such studies are those which deal with the godlike circular movements of the world and the course of the stars, their magnitudes, distances, risings and settings, and the causes of the other appearances in the heavens; and which finally explicate the whole form. For what could be more beautiful than the heavens which contain all beautiful things? Their very names make this clear: *Caelum* (heavens) by naming that which is beautifully carved; and *Mundus* (world), purity and elegance. Many philosophers have called the world a visible god on account of its extraordinary excellence. So if the worth of the arts were measured by the matter with which they deal, this art—which some call astronomy, others astrology, and many of the ancients the consummation of mathematics—would be by far the most outstanding. This art which is as it were the head of all the liberal arts and the one most worthy of a free man leans upon nearly all the other branches of mathematics. Arithmetic, geometry, optics, geodesy, mechanics, and whatever others, all offer themselves in its service. And since a property of all good arts is to draw the mind of man away from the vices and direct it to better things, these arts can do that more plentifully, over and above the unbelievable pleasure of mind [which they furnish]. For who, after applying himself to things which he sees established in the best order and directed by divine ruling, would not through diligent contemplation of them and through a certain habituation be awakened to that which is best and would not wonder at the Artificer of all things, in Whom is all happiness and every good? For the divine Psalmist surely did not say gratuitously that he took pleasure in the workings of god and rejoiced in the works of His hands, unless by means of these things as by some sort of vehicle we are transported to the contemplation of the highest Good.

Page 26: From *Harmonice Mundi* (Harmony of the World)

It has been said in the second book how the regular plane figures are fitted together to form solids; there we spoke of the five regular solids, among others, on account of the plane figures. Nevertheless their number, five, was there demonstrated; and it was added why they were designated by the Platonists as the figures of the world, and to what element any solid was compared on account of what property. But now, in the anteroom of this book, I must speak again concerning these figures, on their own account, not on account of the planes, as much as suffices for the celestial harmonies the reader will find the rest in the *Epitome of Astronomy*, Volume II, Book IV.

Accordingly, from the *Mysterium Cosmographicum*, let me here briefly inculcate the order of the five solids in the world, whereof three are primary and two secondary. For the *cube* is the outmost and most spacious, because firstborn and having the nature [*rationem*] of a *whole*, in the very form of its generation. There follows the *tetrahedron*, as if made a *part*, but cutting up the cube; nevertheless it is primary too, with a solid trilinear angle, like the cube. Within the tetrahedron is the *dodecahedron*, the last of the primary figures, namely, like a solid composed of parts of a cube and similar parts of a tetrahedron, i.e., of irregular tetrahedrons, wherewith the cube inside is roofed over. Next in order is the *icosahedron* on account of its similarity, the last of the secondary figures and having a plurilinear solid angle. The *octahedron* is inmost, which is similar to the cube and the first of the secondary figures and to which as inscriptile the first place is due, just as the first outside place is due to the cube as circumscriptile.

Page 35: From *Epitome Astronomiae Copernicanae* (Epitome of Copernican Astronomy)

By what arguments is it made probable that the primary planets share their own movements around themselves with the secondary planets, and especially the Earth with the Moon?

The Moon and Earth give the first evidence. For, just as above, from the fact that the planets, on drawing near to the Sun, are borne more speedily, we reasoned that the Sun by means of the form from its body, i.e., its form set rotation, moves the planets around itself in the same direction; so also, because we find that in so far as the Moon draws nearer to the Earth—but not to the Sun—so much the more speedily does it move around the Earth, and in the same direction in which the Earth revolves around its axis; it is with the greatest probability that we derive that movement of the moon from the whirling of the Earth; and that is all the more probable, because there is also the correspondence that, just as the rotation of the Sun around its axis is shorter than the shortest period of Mercury, so too the Earth rotates approximately thirty times, before the Moon has one restitution. For if the Moon revolved more quickly than the Earth, its movement could not wholly come from the rotation of the Earth. But belief in this thing is confirmed by the comparison of the four satellites of Jupiter and Jupiter with the six planets and the Sun. For even if in the case of the body of Jupiter we do not have the evidence as to whether it rotates around its axis, which we do have in the case of the terrestrial body and the solar body in particular, that is to say, evidence from the sense-perception. But sense-perception testifies that exactly as it is with the six planets around the Sun, so too is the case with the four satellites of Jupiter: in such fashion that the farther any satellite can digress from Jupiter, the slowlier does it make its return around the body of Jupiter. And that indeed does not occur in the same ratio but in a greater, that is, in the ratio of the 3/2th power of the distance of each planet from Jupiter: and that is exactly the same as the ratio which we found above among the six planets.

LOSSARY

aphelion The point in the orbit of a planet at which it is farthest from the Sun.

armillary sphere An instrument composed of rings showing the positions of important circles of the celestial sphere.

astrology The study of the movement of heavenly bodies with the belief that they influence people's lives.

astronomy The scientific study of space and objects in space.

axis An imaginary straight line passing through the center of a body around which the body rotates.

comet A mass of dirty ice, dust, and gas following a highly elliptical orbit.

cube The product of one number when multiplied by itself three times.

diameter The distance of a straight line passing through the center of an object, usually a sphere.

eclipse Phenomenon that occurs when Earth passes between the Sun and Moon casting a shadow on the Moon (lunar eclipse), or when the Moon passes between the Sun and Earth, casting a shadow on Earth (solar eclipse).

focus One of the two fixed points around which an ellipse is formed.

folio A sheet of any written or printed material.

galaxy A large body of gas, dust, stars, and planets held together by gravity.

gravity A force of attraction between objects.

mean The average of a collection of numbers.

observatory A building designed to house a telescope for the purpose of observing and studying the sky.

orbit The path an object takes as it revolves around another object.

perihelion The point in the orbit of a planet at which it is closest to the Sun.

Platonic solids Shapes that have equal sides and angles, and identical faces.

proportional Having the same ratio.

quadrant An instrument used for measuring altitude.

radius vector The straight line connecting the center of one body to the body that is orbiting around it.

reformer A person who is trying to change an existing system or belief.

sextant An instrument used for measuring angular distances.

square The product of one number when multiplied by itself.

volume The amount of space occupied by an object.

FOR MORE INFORMATION

American Astronomical Society
2000 Florida Ave. NW, Ste. 400
Washington, DC 20009-1231
(202) 328-2010
Web site: http://www.aas.org

Kepler Museum Weil der Stadt
Keplergasse 2
771263 Weil der Stadt
Zimmer 26, Germany
Web site: http://www.kepler-museum.de

NASA Headquarters
Information Center
Washington, DC 20546-0001
(202) 358-0000
Web site: http://www.nasa.gov

The Planetary Science Institute
1700 E. Ft. Lowell Road, Suite 106
Tucson, AZ 85719-2395
(520) 622-6300
e-mail: psikey@psi.edu
Web site: http://www.psi.edu

The University of Arizona
Department of Planetary Sciences
Lunar and Planetary Laboratory
1629 E. University Boulevard
Tucson, AZ 85721-0092
Web site: http://www.lpl.arizona.edu

Web Sites

Due to the changing nature of Internet links, the Rosen
Publishing Group, Inc. has developed an online list of Web
sites related to the subject of this book. This site is updated
regularly. Please use this link to access the list:

http://www.rosenlinks.com/psrsdt/klpm

FOR FURTHER READING

Burnham, Robert, and Gabrielle Walker. *Astronomy*. New York: Reader's Digest Association, 1998.

Couper, Heather, and Nigel Henbest. *How the Universe Works*. London: Dorling Kindersley, 1994.

Ferguson, Kitty. *Tycho & Kepler: The Unlikely Partnership That Forever Changed Our Understanding of the Heavens*. New York: Walker & Company, 2002.

Fradin, Dennis B. *Astronomy*. Chicago: Children's Press, 1986.

Gallant, Roy A. *The Planets: Exploring the Solar System*. New York: Macmillan Publishing Company, 1989.

# BIBLIOGRAPY

Boerst, William J. *Johannes Kepler: Discovering the Laws of Celestial Motion*. Greensboro, NC: Morgan Reynolds Publishing, Inc., 2003.

Ferguson, Kitty. *Tycho & Kepler: The Unlikely Partnership That Forever Changed Our Understanding of the Heavens*. New York: Walker & Company, 2002.

Nicolson, Iain. *Unfolding Our Universe*. Cambridge, England: Cambridge University Press, 1999.

Sullivan, Navin. *Pioneer Astronomers*. New York: The Murray Printing Company, 1964.

PRIMARY SOURCE IMAGE LIST

INDEX

Photo Credits

Front cover, p. 20 © Bettmann/Corbis; title page © Science Photo Library/Photo Researchers, Inc.; pp. 5, 29 Erich Lessing/Art Resource, NY; p. 7 Library of Congress, Prints and Photographs Division; pp. 10, 17, 26, 28, 32, 35, 45 Courtesy of Smithsonian Institution Libraries, Washington, DC; p. 11 © Crawford Library/Royal Observatory, Edinburgh/Photo Researchers, Inc.; pp. 14–15 Walters Art Museum/Bridgeman Art Library; p. 18 Snark/Art Resource, NY; p. 25 Index/Bridgeman Art Library; p. 46 © Archivo Iconografico, S.A./Corbis; p. 49 © Photodisc/Getty Images; p. 51 © Orlicka Galerie, Rychnov nad Kneznou, Czech Republic/Bridgeman Art Library.

About the Author

Heather Hasan graduated from college summa cum laude with a dual major in biochemistry and chemistry. She currently resides in Montgomery County, Maryland, with her husband, Omar, and their son, Samuel.

Editor: Nicholas Croce; Photo Researcher: Jeffrey Wendt